Classroom Activities for Edexcel GCSE Leisure & Tourism

Teacher Guide

Catherine Carden

Edited by Ray Youell

Published by Travel and Tourism Publishing Limited.

Website: www.tandtpublishing.co.uk
Contact: info@tandtpublishing.co.uk

First published 2009

British Library Cataloguing in Publication Data is available
from the British Library on request.

ISBN 9780 9550190 98

Acknowledgements

Thanks to everyone who has supported me in the production
of this book especially Dave, Oliver and Toby who keep me
smiling! My 2008/2009 PGCE Leisure and Tourism group also
deserve a mention as being the reason for me to reflect upon
teaching activities day in, day out and finally thanks to Ray
Youell at Travel and Tourism Publishing for allowing me this
opportunity.

Catherine Carden

Designed and typeset by Sulwyn at Gomer Press
Cover image courtesy of Extreeme Adventure/Travmedia.com
Printed in the UK by Gomer Press, Llandysul

Table of contents

How to use this book

This book supports the Classroom Activities for Edexcel GCSE Leisure and Tourism student book (ISBN 9780955019081) by containing actual or suggested answers for the tasks that the students are asked to complete.

Some answers are definitive, whereas others are suggestions, and alternatives could be as relevant. There are some tasks where answers are not given – students' responses will vary greatly and these are left to the teacher's discretion in their own particular circumstances.

The book is split into the 4 units of the Edexcel GCSE qualification and then by topic area. It has been designed to be used in the classroom as well as for self-study and homework. There are individual activities as well as paired and group work.

Students write the majority of their answers directly into their books, so there is little need for additional paper or books. Some tasks require students to produce a poster or presentation, for example, and for these they will need additional paper or access to ICT equipment.

After they have completed the tasks for each unit, students can use this book as a method of revision for the externally assessed units or to help with their internally assessed pieces of work.

Sample assessment materials (and answers) are included for the 4 GCSE units. These are provided as an extra source of practice for students before completing their actual tests and controlled assessments. Teachers will need to refer to the published mark schemes from Edexcel when assessing some of the tasks.

The book includes a grid to highlight all the skills that students are using whilst carrying out each activity, showing how they are developing skills alongside their subject knowledge.

About tandtONLine

Everybody who buys this book can register for free access to tandtONLine (standing for travel & tourism online) – a unique web-based teaching & learning resource for travel and tourism staff and students. It gives you a host of extra features that are regularly updated by academic staff and industry experts, including:

- The latest news from the travel and tourism industry;
- Key statistics on UK, European and global tourism;
- Glossary of common terms and key definitions;
- Links to useful websites;
- Extra staff teaching resources linked to textbooks.

Register by going to **www.tandtonline.co.uk** and completing the online registration form using the unique book code found on the inside back cover of this book.

 **The leisure and tourism industry**

Topic 1.1: The nature of the leisure and tourism industry

Activity 1a

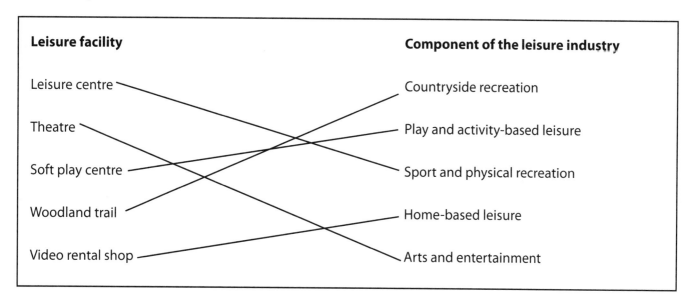

Activity 1b

- Countryside recreation
- Play and activity-based leisure
- Sport and physical recreation
- Home-based leisure
- Arts and entertainment

e.g. boating lake, trim trails
e.g. play park
e.g. gym, health club
e.g. computer game shop
e.g. cinema

Activity 1c

Answers could include: Countryside recreation (local council leisure department, Forestry Commission); play and activity-based leisure (Center Parcs, PGL); sport and physical recreation (David Lloyd Leisure, Fitness First); home-based leisure (Game, W H Smith); arts & entertainment (Odeon, Gala Bingo).

Activity 2a – 2c

Component (A)	Product or service (B)	Company (C)
Travel agents	Selling package holidays, car hire, etc.	e.g. Thomas Cook, First Choice, etc.
Tour operators	Putting together package holidays	e.g. Kuoni, Thomson Holidays, etc.
Tourist information	Providing information to visitors	e.g. VisitBritain, Visit Wales, etc.
Online travel services	Comparing prices of travel insurance	e.g. Expedia, lastminute.com, etc.
Accommodation and catering	Hotel rooms	e.g. Hilton, Travelodge, etc.
Transportation	Train services	e.g. Eurostar, Virgin Trains, etc.

Activity 3a

This task will generate a range of students' own experiences. Some teacher input to suggest that 'attractions' can be both built and natural may be helpful. Also, the fact that many attractions were built for other purposes, but have since become popular with visitors, e.g. cathedrals, parliament buildings, castles, etc.

Activity 3b

The location of the destinations is shown on the map below:

Activity 3c

Country	Attraction name	Built or natural?
USA	Grand Canyon	Natural
France	Eiffel Tower	Built
Australia	Bondi Beach	Natural
Italy	Leaning Tower of Pisa	Built
Zambia/Zimbabwe border	Victoria Falls	Natural
USA	Universal Studios	Built
Russia	The Kremlin	Built
England	Buckingham Palace	Built
France, Switzerland & Italy	The Alps	Natural

Activity 4a

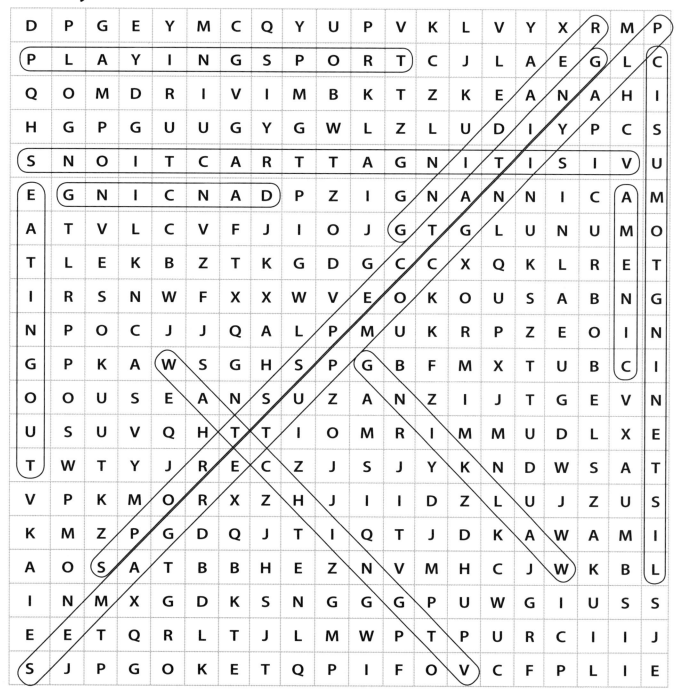

Students should complete the wordsearch as shown on page 3, finding these words – playing computer games, reading, cinema, listening to music, dancing, eating out, sports spectating, watching TV, walking, visiting attractions, playing sport.

Activity 4b

Students must produce tally tables showing a range of leisure activities. Carrying out the survey could be an individual or group activity.

Activity 4c

The students' bar charts will vary depending on the results of their surveys.

Activity 4d

Initially, students' interpretation of their survey results is expected to be descriptive, highlighting the most and least popular activities, but then move on to be a little more analytical, suggesting reasons for popularity of activities, e.g. existence of nearby facilities, interest in health and fitness, government initiatives, etc.

Activity 5a

Students will choose a minimum of 5 facilities and a maximum of 9 leisure facilities from the list given, providing a relevant justification for each, e.g. growing popularity of this type of facility, likely demand from local population, etc.

Activity 5b

Students will list the facilities they have chosen <u>not</u> to include in Albany New Town and include relevant reasons for so doing, e.g. insufficient demand from the local population.

Activity 5c

Students will locate each of their chosen facilities on the New Town plan. Class discussion is a useful way to help decide on ideal locations. A blank map of Albany New Town is included on page 5 to aid you in this discussion.

Activity 5d

This task could be linked to a group visit or following a guest speaker's presentation. Students' projects will need to cover the following points:

i.   A description of the location of their chosen leisure facility, e.g. map, proximity to other amenities, transport links, etc.
ii. An explanation of why they think it has been located there, e.g. close to residential areas, joint use with schools, etc.
iii. A description of the main activities and services available at the chosen leisure facility, e.g. programme of activities, ancillary facilities (food outlets, retail), etc.
iv. Suggestions of how they think the chosen facility could be improved, e.g. wider range of activities, better equipment, longer opening hours, etc.

Albany New Town

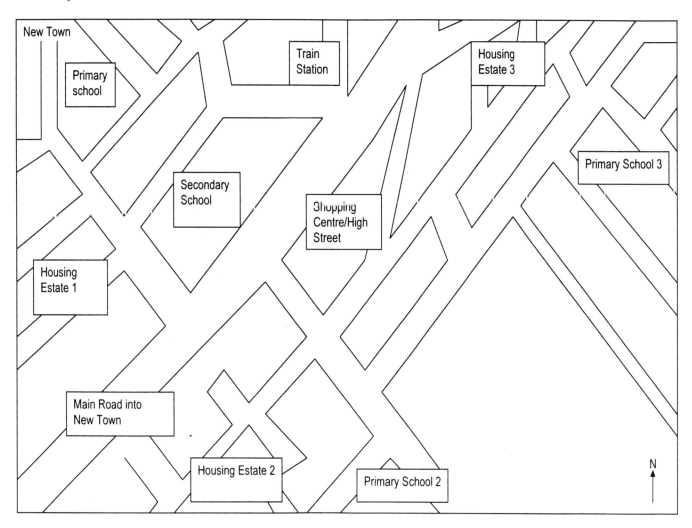

Activity 6a

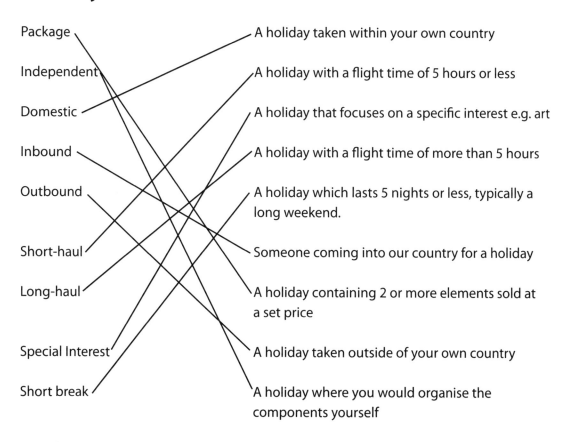

Package	A holiday taken within your own country
Independent	A holiday with a flight time of 5 hours or less
Domestic	A holiday that focuses on a specific interest e.g. art
Inbound	A holiday with a flight time of more than 5 hours
Outbound	A holiday which lasts 5 nights or less, typically a long weekend.
Short-haul	Someone coming into our country for a holiday
Long-haul	A holiday containing 2 or more elements sold at a set price
Special Interest	A holiday taken outside of your own country
Short break	A holiday where you would organise the components yourself

Activity 6b

This task will have varying student answers. It is key that the students can provide a FULL description of the type(s) of holiday.

Activity 6c

Type of holiday	Example
Package	A 7-night holiday with Thomson to Benidorm for £350 per person, including flights, accommodation and transfers.
Independent	A backpacking tour of the Greek Islands where the hotel was booked online, the flights were booked with easyJet, the boat tickets bought in Athens and the hotel booked on arrival.
Domestic	A family travelling on holiday from London to Cornwall for a week in a mobile home.
Inbound	A couple from Japan honeymooning in Edinburgh.
Outbound	A group of friends spending a week in Ibiza.
Short-haul	A businessman travelling for a meeting in Brussels.
Long-haul	A couple going away to get married in the Maldives.
Special interest	A group of friends setting off for a painting holiday in Tuscany.
Short break	A stag weekend (Fri – Mon) in Barcelona.

Activity 7a

Leisure centre assistant: (1) To maintain health and safety in the leisure centre; (2) To deal with customer enquiries.
Fitness instructor: (1) To induct people into the gym when they first join, showing them how to use the equipment; (2) To write individual exercise plans for customers.
Lifeguard: (1) To maintain health and safety in and around the pool/beach area; (2) To provide first aid to swimmers when needed.
Park ranger: (1) To provide information to visitors; (2) To monitor wildlife and plant habitats in the parks.
Cinema staff: (1) To sell tickets to customers to see the films on offer; (2) To show people to their seats in the cinema.

Activity 7b

Students' posters must meet the following criteria stated in the task:

i.   Find a job advert/s for your chosen job;
ii. Using the information in the advert, produce a poster which will be displayed at a careers fair for school leavers giving more information about your chosen job. You will need to include information such as main duties, the skills and qualities needed for the job, the expected salary, qualifications required as well as any further information that you feel is important.

The magazine *Leisure Opportunities* www.leisureopportunities.co.uk is a useful source of information on jobs in leisure and tourism, as is the website www.travelmole.com (registration required for full access).

Activity 7c

Students will clearly identify one job and give a detailed explanation as to how this best matches them in terms of their skills, qualities and qualifications.

Activity 8a

The answers to the crossword are as follows.

Across

5. Travel clerk
6. Coach driver

Down

1. Tourism call centre staff
2. Guides
3. Air cabin crew
4. Resort representatives
5. Tourist information centre staff

Activity 8b

Students must produce a 3-minute presentation which covers the following points concerning one of the jobs in the crossword:

i.   The job title;

ii.   The main duties and responsibilities of this job role;

iii. The skills and qualities needed for the job;

iv.   Any qualifications that are required;

v.   Some example companies that they could work for.

The magazine *Leisure Opportunities* www.leisureopportunities.co.uk is a useful source of information on jobs in leisure and tourism, as is the website www.travelmole.com (registration required for full access).

Activity 8c

Students will identify one job that they would like to do in the tourism industry and explain why they would like to do this. It is expected that they will refer to how their own skills and qualities relate well to the job, as well as giving more general reasons such as the ability to travel (if appropriate), the chance to deal with people face-to-face, opportunities for promotion, keeping fit while working, etc.

Topic 1.2: Introduction to business operations in leisure and tourism

Activity 1a

Human resources (HR) are responsible for the recruitment and development of personnel that work within the company, as well as issuing contracts of employment, staff training, interviewing and advising on staff working conditions.

Information technology (IT) is responsible for the installation of ICT systems, maintenance of ICT systems, programming and dealing with ICT problems.

Finance is responsible for the business accounts, income, expenditure, paying creditors and calling in money from debtors.

Sales and marketing are responsible for promoting the business within an agreed budget. They will also be responsible for monitoring sales and putting measures in place to increase income.

Administration is responsible for the smooth operation of clerical tasks, dealing with paperwork, receiving and distributing correspondence.

Activity 2a

i.   To increase sales, increase profits, increase market share, decrease costs, maximise revenue, etc.

ii. To become the 'greenest', environmentally-friendly airline, to support local and national charities, to develop a high profile image, etc.

Activity 2b

Aims and objectives will vary amongst students, but could include: (1) To increase membership numbers; (2) To offer up-to-date equipment and training methods; (3) To maximise profits; (4) To support the local community and the government health agenda; (5) To offer excellent customer service; (6) To provide a safe and secure environment for staff and customers.

Activity 3

a.   Longleat has introduced new products in order to offer visitors another reason for making a return visit to the attraction. New products also help to widen the 'customer base', i.e. encourage different types of visitors to come to Longleat. Ultimately, the introduction of new products helps Longleat compete for business with similar attractions in the UK.

b.   For 2009, Longleat is open from 4th April to the 1st of November. The attraction closes for the remainder of the year as there is insufficient demand from visitors to make it financially worthwhile to open. The winter closure also gives time for maintenance, refurbishment and the introduction of new products.

c.   The 2009 passport ticket prices are £23 for adults, £15 for children (3-14 years) and £17 for senior citizens (60+ years). These prices are competitive with many similar stately home attractions, e.g. Woburn's 2009 passport ticket prices are £22.50 for adults, £15.50 for children (3-15 years) and £19 for senior citizens. Like all visitor attractions, Longleat regularly reviews its admission prices in order to remain competitive.

d.   Having the passport ticket valid for the whole season encourages people to visit more than once. This generates more 'secondary spending' in areas such as catering outlets, gift shops, etc, thereby increasing the overall income for the attraction.

e. Longleat attracts a wide variety of visitors, who together make up its 'market'. These include families, coach parties, school and college students, overseas visitors, senior citizens, etc. The managers at Longleat must ensure that the attraction caters for the needs of all these types of visitors if it is to remain successful.

f. PR (public relations) involves all types of activities that are not paid advertising, but are designed to raise awareness of an attraction and increase sales, for example sponsorship of events and charities, hosting journalists' visits, television programmes (Longleat is currently the location for BBC's Animal Park), local radio interviews, issuing press releases about new developments at the attraction, signage on vehicles, uniforms, logos, etc.

Activity 4a

What Is the Malintent device designed to do? It is a device to fight against terrorism. It can read a traveller's temperature, mind, heart rate and respiration.

The inventors suggest additional benefits to the device. What are these? Cut queuing times at airports and put an end to the current ban on carrying liquids on aircraft.

Some people have concerns that the system is overly invasive and a breach of privacy. What are your views on this? Students will have their own views – this is an ideal discussion point about personal privacy, the threat of terrorism on travel and tourism, etc.

Activity 4b

Students will identify how technology could be used in the hotel. For each type of technology, students must identify and describe ways in which it could be used to cover the key areas identified, i.e. ensure safety and security of the hotel, its guests and staff, to store data and bookings made, to market and promote the hotel and to confirm and remind people of their bookings and payments due.

The Internet, broadband and e-mail: e.g. e-mail reminders to customers, new website for the hotel, e-mail system for staff communication, wi-fi access, etc.

Computerised records, electronic databases: e.g. customer database, staff database, direct mail sent from information stored on customer database, etc.

Mobile 'phones, WAP: e.g. reminder of booking on mobile phone (text), alerts of special offers and promotions, etc.

Electronic security, health and safety, ID measures: e.g. CCTV, staff identity badges, key cards for rooms, electronic safes in rooms, etc.

Activity 5a

i. To enable the business to grow, generate repeat business, increase sales and profits, develop a sustainable business, etc.

ii. Provide excellent customer service, offer discounts and sales incentives, provide good communication, listen to customer feedback, introduce new products, stage events, develop staff training prgrammes, etc.

iii. To grow their business, increase market share, increase sales and profits, do better than their competitors, reward staff, etc.

iv. Advertising, special offers, mailshots to local areas, free gifts, 'two-for-one' promotions, tie-ins with local media, etc.

v. Listen to customer feedback, monitor the market, carry out market research, develop and sell new products, provide excellent levels of customer service, increase staff training, incentivise staff with rewards, bonuses, etc.

Activity 5a(vi)

Credit crunch: less money to spend on 'luxuries' (i.e. lower disposable income), fall in bookings for expensive holidays, increase in domestic holidays in the UK, less business travel, etc.

Increased oil prices: increased flight prices, decrease in air travel, increase in rail and sea travel, increased price of petrol and so less touring holidays by car, increase in UK holidays closer to home, etc.

A terrorist attack on US aircraft: decreased travel for leisure and business, avoidance of the destinations targeted, increased domestic tourism, etc.

Terrorist attack on the London Underground system: decrease in incoming tourism to the UK, decrease in day trips to London, increased use of other transport methods, etc.

Poor exchange rate for the Euro (making countries that use the Euro expensive for us when visiting): increased domestic tourism, decrease in tourism to Eurozone countries (countries that use the Euro), increase in tourism to countries where the £ is strong, increase in travel to non-Eurozone countries, e.g. Turkey, etc.

Poor summer weather in the UK: increase in outbound holidays, decrese in domestic holidays, decrese in incoming tourism, etc.

Activity 5b

Students choose one external factor from those in Actvity 5a(vi) to Investigate further as a group and then produce a presentation on this, which must be factual, clear and concise.

Activities 6a – 6e

Working in groups, students are given an area of legislation to investigate relating to one of the following:

1. Employeees, e.g. the use of display screen equipment at work (computer monitors);
2. Customers, e.g. hazards in swimming pools;
3. Property, e.g. storage of hazardous materials in the workplace;
4. Health and hygiene, e.g. food safety in restaurants.

Students must agree a plan, carry out research, collate their findings and make a presentation to the rest of the class.

The Health and Safety Executive's website www.hse.gov.uk is a useful source of information on health and safety in leisure and tourism.

Topic 1.3: Factors influencing customer choice

Activity 1

a. A leisure facility is a place that offers leisure activities for the general public or on a private membership basis. Examples include swimming pools, sports centres, fitness clubs, health resorts, night clubs, country parks, outdoor activity centres, etc.
b. Students' lists will vary depending on their own particular circumstances. They could be prompted to consider 'leisure facilities' in their widest sense (see answers to Activity 1c).
c. *Health*: leisure centre, spa, swimming pool, etc.
   Fitness: gym, health club, country park, etc.

Relaxation: sauna, spa, beauty therapy centre, etc.
Entertainment: cinema, theatre, circus, etc.
Spiritual wellbeing: alternative therapy centre, spa, yoga classes, etc.
Challenge: outdoor activities centre, paintball centre, go kart track, etc.
Social opportunities: e.g. restaurant, pub, nightclub, etc.

Activity 2

a. Students' responses will vary depending on their own particular circumstances.
b. Unjumbled words are: holidays, sightseeing, visiting tourist attractions, visiting friends and relatives, business travel, educational purposes.
c. Students must match the reason for travel to the relevant scenario, as follows:

i. Holiday;
ii. Educational purposes;
iii. Visiting friends and relatives;
iv. Sightseeing;
v. Visiting tourist attractions;
vi. Business travel.

Activity 3a

Students complete the wordsearch as shown on below, finding these words – air, road, rail, sea.

N	Q	L	V	R	S	A	A	Y	A
Y	V	J	S	K	W	Z	S	I	W
I	J	H	B	F	S	U	N	D	R
B	P	P	O	D	O	M	D	Z	G
T	L	D	A	B	R	W	V	F	A
R	O	A	D	U	M	D	W	U	H
M	M	Y	U	J	C	Y	S	L	D
R	R	E	U	Q	B	K	I	S	I
K	Y	K	L	E	U	A	W	E	L
E	W	P	P	B	R	K	W	A	M

Activity 3b

Air	Scheduled air service	British Airways
Road	Coach	National Express
Rail	High-speed train	Eurostar
Sea	Ferry	P&O

Activity 4a

Students are asked to identify factors they consider when choosing a method of transport e.g. cost, time, comfort, speed, ease of booking, safety, security, frequency of services, etc.

Activity 4b

i.   Availability, cost, convenience, time of travel, length of journey, etc.
ii. Speed, availability, access to starting point of journey, etc.
iii. Speed, availability, frequency, destination routes, suitable timetables, access to business facilities, etc.
iv. Speed, availability, frequency, cost, etc.

Activity 4c

i.   Eurostar;
ii. Aircraft;
iii. Coach;
iv. Car and ferry;
v.   Car.

Topic 1.4: Introduction to destinations, impacts and sustainability

Activity 1a

i.   *Seaside resorts*: e.g. Brighton, Skegness, Blackpool, Margate, Bournemouth;
ii. *Countryside areas*: e.g. Pembrokeshire Coast National Park, Peak District National Park, Jurassic Coast, Dorset, the Cotswolds;
iii. *Tourist towns and cities*: e.g. London, York, Canterbury, Edinburgh, Cambridge;
iv. *Business travel destinations*: e.g. Blackpool, Manchester, Cardiff, Belfast, Brighton;
v.   *Purpose-built destinations* e.g. Butlin's Bognor Regis, Center Parcs Sherwood Forest;
vi. *Historical and cultural destinations*: e.g. Stonehenge, York, Stratford-upon-Avon.

Activity 1b

Students should accurately locate and label their chosen destinations on the blank UK map in their books. Locations will differ based on their answers to Activity 1a.

Activity 1c

Students choose one destination from those selected in Activity 1a and produce a poster to advertise this destination, which must include key tourist information as well as images.

Activity 2

a. A group of people living in a particular location. In the case of tourism, the community is made up of the people living in the tourist destination, sometimes referred to as the 'host community'.

b. An effect of a particular occurrence, which can be either negative, positive or both. For example, the impacts of opening a new air route to a tourist resort are likely to include more income for hotel owners, but could cause more congestion on beaches.

c. Jobs, more leisure facilities for local people and tourists, improved infrastructure (roads, airports, ports, communications), more income for local businesses, etc.

d. Increased prices, congestion, vandalism, poor behaviour, overcrowding, destruction of wildlife habitats, etc.

e. Students are to produce a model or 3-D poster to show both the positive and negative impacts that tourism can have upon a community. This can be made using boxes and other suitable materials. They should consider their anwers to Activity 2a – 2d when completing this task.

Activity 3

a. Answers could include congestion, wear and tear, erosion, visual pollution, air pollution, noise pollution, increased money for conservation, increased awareness of the environment, cleaner beaches, more income for environmental businesses, creation of jobs, etc.

b. Students must sort the impacts they identified in Activity 3a into those that are positive and those that are negative.

c. Each students' letter will be different, depending on their own ideas and experiences. It is expected that they will include negative impacts from the table they completed for Activity 3b.

Activity 4a & 4b

The group should work together to discover important points about ecotourism and agree a defintion. The International Ecotourism Society defines 'ecotourism' as *responsible travel to natural areas that conserves the environment and improves the well-being of local people*. The Society's ecotourism principles are:

- *Minimise impact;*
- *Build environmental and cultural awareness and respect;*
- *Provide positive experiences for both visitors and hosts;*
- *Provide direct financial benefits for conservation;*
- *Provide financial benefits and empowerment for local people;*
- *Raise sensitivity to host communities' political, environmental and social climate.*

Activity 4c

The work produced from this task will vary greatly and be individual to the student group. It must reflect the points discovered during the completion of Activities 4a and 4b, as well as from more general research into eco-friendly accommodation. Students' work is to be presented as a web page or brochure page featuring the guest house, aimed at tempting vsitors to make a reservation.

Activity 4d

The World Commission on Environment and Development defines 'sustainable development' as *meeting the needs of the present without compromising the ability of future generations to meet their own needs*. Students should explain in their own words what they understand by the term and give examples.

Activity 4e

i.   Tourism is a great contributor to the national economy and social well-being of the country. DCMS wishes to see that UK tourism develops in a way that is respectful of the environment and the communities where tourism takes place.

ii. The tourism industry may develop in a way that is unsustainable, i.e. that is harmful to the environment and local communities.

iii. Through publications, advice and guidance to tourism businesses, conferences, research into sustainable tourism, etc.

Activity 5

Students complete this task as a class. The completed display must:

i.   Describe the Olympic plan for London (to include pictures, maps and descriptions of sites and developments);

ii. Explain how the development is 'sustainable', i.e. benefits locals, visitors, tourists and the environment;

iii. Explain why sustainability is important for this project.

The following website is a useful source of further information for this task www.london2012.com.

Unit 2 Sales, promotion and operations in leisure and tourism

Topic 2.1: Sales in leisure and tourism contexts

Activity 1

a. Students are asked to identify a range of relevant selling situations, such as:

- In a travel agency
- A holiday call centre
- Hotel reception
- Theatre box office
- Cinema foyer
- On board a cruise ship
- At a leisure centre reception
- A golf driving range

a. Unjumbled words are: administration, finance, human resources, regional office.
b. Students could work in groups for this task. Also, a visit to a leisure and tourism facility, or presentation from a guest speaker, would add realism. Students choose a leisure or tourism organisation and must research the 3 topics given in their books. Their findings are to be presented as a short written report.

Activity 2

Students choose a local leisure and tourism organisation to investigate as a group. This could be a hotel, leisure centre, health club, cinema, museum, etc. The aim is to produce the marketing mix for their chosen organisation, presented as a poster. The posters must include information on the four Ps – product, price, place and promotion – as detailed in their books. A study visit or guest speaker from an organisation could provide useful information for this task.

Topic 2.2: Promotion in leisure and tourism contexts

Activity 1a

Segment	Company or product	Target market
Age	Club 18-30	18–30 year olds
Gender	Spa resort	Females
Social group	Private jets	Socio-economic group A
Lifestyle	Online check-in	Business travellers
Ethnicity	BBC Asian Network	Asian community
Geographical location	Local cinema	People in the town and surrounding areas

Activities 1b – 1d

Students choose a market segment and then a target market from within this segment (these should be different from those included in the chart in Activity 1a). They design a holiday that is aimed at their chosen market and write full details of the holiday (location, features, travel arrangements, price, etc.) in the space provided in their book. Access to holiday brochures and websites of holiday companies will be useful for this task. Students should not simply duplicate an existing holiday product, but use existing material to devise their own.

Activity 2

a. Answers are likely to include: good design, information provided, suitability for the target market, use of colour, use of graphics, text and images, personality endorsements, etc.
b. Students need to be given a range of promotional materials for different leisure and tourism products, services and companies (brochures, leaflets, advertisements, direct mail flyers, printouts of web pages, etc.). They must evaluate each of these using the following criteria:

i. Design;
ii. Information provided;
iii. Suitability for the target market.

   Evaluations must be produced on a poster, containing the piece of promotional material (where possible).
c. Students are to choose a leisure or tourism product/service/event or company and produce a piece of promotional material for this. They need to consider the points covered in Activities 2a and 2b when completing this task.

Topic 2.3: Promotional techniques and materials in leisure and tourism

Activity 1

a. Students should complete the wordsearch as shown on page 17, finding these promotional techniques used in leisure and tourism – advertising, direct marketing, public relations, displays, sponsorship, demonstrations, sales promotions.
b. Students are given a scenario of working in a local B & B. The owners need to promote the business more and have asked the student to help by choosing 3 different promotional techniques that could help them achieve this. They should refer to the items in the previous wordsearch to help them complete this task, giving explanations and justifications for their choices.
c. Divide the class into groups and give each group an example of a promotional technique (refer to the previous wordsearch for examples). Each group must identify the advantages and disadvantages of their promotional technique, when used in leisure and tourism.

Activity 2a

This activity focuses on promotional MATERIALS, not promotional TECHNIQUES, e.g. a press release is an example of a promotional material, but public relations (PR) is the technique. Answers will vary, but could include brochures, t-shirts, printed balloons, press releases, flyers, website advertisements, printed mouse mats, newspaper advertisements, printed pens, etc.

G	S	I	X	O	W	S	U	S	L	N	A	X	R	M
U	N	C	H	G	W	N	V	A	D	O	D	J	H	I
P	O	I	X	F	E	O	O	L	R	X	V	F	E	X
P	I	M	T	R	Q	I	U	E	W	U	E	X	G	U
L	T	B	U	E	G	T	W	S	H	S	R	S	B	E
L	A	E	D	W	K	A	E	P	D	H	T	Y	Q	E
E	L	G	U	W	X	R	T	R	I	E	I	A	K	C
V	E	O	C	T	C	T	A	O	L	P	S	L	H	P
Q	R	B	U	P	K	S	U	M	B	Y	I	P	H	U
L	C	W	O	Z	T	N	E	O	T	W	N	S	L	O
S	I	Y	T	L	U	O	Q	T	Y	C	G	I	Y	H
N	L	M	H	S	B	M	L	I	T	P	E	D	W	C
B	B	C	J	S	B	E	Z	O	M	L	S	R	P	A
T	U	H	N	N	V	D	V	N	Y	H	I	U	I	T
Z	P	P	I	H	S	R	O	S	N	O	P	S	M	D

Activity 2b

This should be presented by students as a press release, which should highlight the fact that the agency has been voted *TTG Agent of the Year*. The release should have a catchy headline and include positive information about why the agency won the award, e.g. excellent customer service standards, good financial performance, a wide range of holiday and travel products on offer, etc. Key points when writing press releases include: (1) Keep it crisp, factual and informative; (2) Write to suit the style of the publication; (3) Answer the basic questions of who, what, when, where, why as early as possible, preferably in the first 2 paragraphs; (4) Get the main news point into the first paragraph; (5) Give a date to the release; (6) Include full details of a contact person at the end.

Activity 2c

Students are to choose a leisure or tourism company that is currently running an advertising campaign (this can be local or national). Students are to spend a week noting down all the different promotional materials that it uses in its campaign. Students will need access to the Internet and a variety of printed media to complete this task. They should also be encouraged to make note of any relevant TV and radio advertisements that they come across outside of school time.

Activity 2d

Students' answers will vary depending on which promotional materials feature in their different advertising campaigns.

Activity 3a

The answer to this question should be 'no', based on the fact that promotional techniques and materials can be expensive – companies have to work within budgets to get the best value from the techniques and materials they use. Also, companies have to bear in mind the characteristics of the people they are trying to reach (the target market). Not all techniques and materials are suitable for every target market. For example, advertisements for expensive cruises are unlikely to be placed in newspapers whose readers have low income levels.

Activity 3b

i.   Students' answers should include examples based around cost, placement and target market;
ii. Students' answers should include examples based around placement and target market;
iii. Students' answers should include examples based around placement, cost and target market.

Topic 2.4: Operations used in leisure and tourism organisations

Activity 1

i.   Overseas call centres and administration

The impacts on the *company* will be: (1) Cheaper rent for office space; (2) Lower wage costs; (3) Need for new staff training.
The impacts on the *employees* will be: (1) Possible redundancies for UK staff; (2) Career opportunities for overseas staff.
The impacts on the *customer* will be: (1) Possible language barriers when communicating.

ii. The growth in home working

The impacts on the *company* will be: (1) Reduction in office space needed; (2) Difficulty contacting and meeting with staff; (3) Reduction in costs.
The impacts on the *employees* will be: (1) Increased flexibility; (2) Greater motivation; (3) Lack of employee/colleague support.
The impacts on the *customer* will be: (1) Absence of a central base to contact the company; (2) Restricted contact times.

iii. Online reservation systems

The impacts on the *company* will be: (1) Reduction in staff costs; (2) Extra training needed for staff; (3) Increase in profits; (4) Change in employee numbers.
The impacts on the *employees* will be: (1) Reduction in employee numbers (redundancy); (2) Staff possibly deployed in other areas of the company.
The impacts on the *customer* will be: (1) Greater flexibility; (2) 24-hour access to systems.

iv. Online check-in for transport services

The impacts on the *company* will be: (1) Reduction in staff costs; (2) Investment costs for new equipment; (3) Speedier check-in process; (4) Increased profits.
The impacts on the *employees* will be: (1) Reduction in employee numbers (redundancy); (2) Staff possibly deployed in other areas of the company.
The impacts on the *customer* will be: (1) Faster check-in; (2) Fewer front-line staff to offer help when needed.

v. E-brochures and 'virtual tours'

The impacts on the *company* will be: (1) Possible increased sales; (2) Increased set-up costs for the organisation; (3) Decrease in profits initially; (4) Extra training for staff needed.
The impacts on the *employees* will be: (1) Training needs.
The impacts on the *customer* will be: (1) More information available; (2) Greater convenience; (3) Clearer information.

Activity 2

Students are given the following scenario:

It has been decided by BAA (British Airports Authority) that ALL check-in must be done online, as BAA moves to streamline its busy airports. You work for a major airline that flies out of the key BAA airports. This announcement obviously has important implications for your airline as the company is going to have to make significant changes to accommodate online check-in services.

Working in a small group, students must consider the economic (money-related) impacts on the airline of this decision. They need to look at how the decision will affect the following (thinking long-term and short-term)

i.   *The profits of the airline* – these are likely to fall in the short-term, as investment will be needed in changes to equipment, IT systems, extra staff training, etc. In the long-term, profits are likely to rise, given that the company will save staff costs through employing fewer members of staff.
ii. *The airline's costs* – these will increase in the short-term, to pay for new equipment, IT systems, staff training, etc. In the long-term, the company's overall costs will fall, since it will benefit from smaller numbers of staff needed for check-in.

Activity 3

Students are given the scenario of working in the reservations department of a large tour operator. Recently the company has reviewed new technologies and business systems, as well as its current ways of working. The management has issued a statement in its annual report concerning the introduction of a new online booking system, moving its call centre to Mumbai in India and making changes to ensure that its customers are cared for more in its resorts and at airports.

Students must read the statement and, as a group, discuss the implications that these decisions are going to have on employment within the company. These are likely to include – loss of jobs in the high street stores, loss of jobs with the closure of the London-based call centre, possible redeployment of staff in new roles in resorts and at airports, the need for extra staff training, etc.

Groups are to present their conclusions to the rest of the class.

 **Unit 3** **The leisure and tourism environment**

Topic 3.1: A dynamic industry

Activity 1

Students (in groups) are given one of the following factors to investigate:

- Development of home-based leisure, e.g. virtual reality games;
- Growth in home cinemas and digital TV;
- Use of global positioning system (GPS) technology;
- Use of MP3 technology;
- Demand for podcasts;
- Growth in ticketless travel and e-tickets;
- Use of automated check-in facilities;
- Rise in home computer ownership.

Each group must carry out some research on their topic and make a presentation to the rest of the class. This must cover:

a. A description of the factor;
b. An explanation of the influence of the factor;
c. An analysis of how the factor has led to change in the leisure and tourism industry;
d. An analysis of how the factor has led to the development of new products and services.

Activity 2

Students will put forward a variety of answers, which could include the following:

a. Spa resorts, 5-star hotels, eco-tours, eco-friendly holidays, long-haul travel, activity holidays, adventure travel, informal cruising, etc.
b. Changing tastes of consumers, escape from the demands at work and home, the chance to experience something different, to explore new cultures, to try something different in their leisure time, thrill-seeking, etc.
c. Nintendo Wii, home cinema systems, digital satellite and terrestrial TV, music downloads, computer games consoles, gardening equipment, outdoor leisure equipment (trampolines), etc.
d. People are becoming more adventurous in their leisure time, taking more short breaks throughout the year, spending more time outdoors, taking on leisure activities often seen abroad (barbeque areas in forest areas, sea canoeing), etc.
e. Short breaks in the UK, short breaks abroad, long-haul city breaks (Rio de Janiero, Cape Town, Hong Kong), etc.
f. A person normally over the age of 60 who uses the Internet for a variety of purposes, including researching things to do in his/her leisure time.
g. 'Soft adventure' activities (walking, orienteering, sailing, cycling, keep fit, etc.), second homes abroad, timeshare developments, cruising, activities linked to hobbies such as painting, gardening, craft work, wood work, etc.
h. Families with young children.
i. More relaxed and informal cruising, cheaper cruise holidays, different destinations on offer, more cruises starting and finishing at UK ports, new activities on board cruise ships, for example climbing walls, artificial surfing, fitness suites, etc.

Activity 3

Students (in groups) are given one of the following events to investigate:

- The global credit crunch and recession, e.g. from 2008 onwards;

- Impact of increased cost of fuel/inflation, e.g. increased oil prices 2007 – 2008;

- Acts of terrorism, e.g. September 11th 2001;

- Natural disasters, e.g. tsunami, floods, avalanches, hurricanes, tornadoes, earthquakes;

- Changes in exchange rates, e.g. £ versus $, £ versus Euro;

- Accidents/injury to customers, e.g. the recent death of children in Greek holiday accommodation after carbon monoxide poisoning.

Each group must produce an informative poster that covers the following:

a. Examples of situations related to their event, including articles where appropriate;

b. Identification, with explanations, of the changes and impacts that have occurred within the leisure and tourism industry as a result of the event.

Topic 3.2: UK tourist destinations

Activity 1

a. Students locate the destinations on the outline map of the UK as shown on page 22.

b. Students must describe the location of each destination as part of a written report. This should emphasise the geographical features of destinations, e.g. in a coastal area, mountain region, close to centres of population, expanses of water, etc.

c. Students must shade each destination with the correct colour as follows (please note that some destinations can fall into more than one category, e.g. Brighton is both a seaside resort and a business travel destination, but only one category has been chosen for this task):

- Blue (seaside resorts) = Oban, Portrush, Llandudno, Blackpool, Whitby, Great Yarmouth, Newquay, Eastbourne;

- Green (countryside areas) = Loch Lomond and the Trossachs, Antrim Coast & Glens, Snowdonia, Lake District, Yorkshire Dales, Cotswolds, Dartmoor, New Forest;

- Brown (tourist towns and cities) = Glasgow, Bangor, Conwy, Liverpool, York, Warwick, Oxford, Cambridge;

- Red (business travel destinations) = Edinburgh, Belfast, Cardiff, Manchester, Leeds, Birmingham, London, Brighton;

- Grey (purpose-built destinations) = Aviemore, Galgorm Resort, Celtic Manor Resort, Keldy Forest Holidays, Sherwood Forest Center Parcs, Longleat Forest Center Parcs, Alton Towers Resort, Butlins – Bognor Regis;

- Yellow (historical and cultural destinations) = St Andrews, Londonderry, St Davids, Chester, Lindisfarne, Stratford-upon-Avon, Bath, Canterbury.

d. Students complete the table as follows:

Tourist board region	Destinations for which they are responsible
Northern Ireland Tourist Board	Portrush, Antrim Coast and Glens, Belfast, Galgorm Resort, Bangor, Londonderry.
Scottish Tourist Board	Oban, Loch Lomond and the Trossachs, Glasgow, Edinburgh, Aviemore, St Andrews.
Visit Wales	Llandudno, Snowdonia, Conwy, Cardiff, Celtic Manor Resort, St Davids.
Visit England and England's North Country	Blackpool, Whitby, Lake District, Yorkshire Dales, Liverpool, York, Manchester, Leeds, Chester, Lindisfarne, Keldy Forest holidays.
Visit England and Heart of England	Birmingham, Warwick, Alton Towers Resort, Stratford-upon-Avon.
Visit England and East Midlands	Great Yarmouth, Cambridge, Sherwood Forest Center Parcs.
Visit England and London	London.
Visit England and South East	Eastbourne, Canterbury, Oxford, Brighton, the New Forest, Butlins – Bognor Regis.
Visit England and South West	Newquay, Dartmoor, Bath, Longleat Forest Center Parcs, Cotswolds.

e. Students are required to produce a leaflet about UK destinations. The leaflet needs to include the specific features (climate, natural attractions, built attractions, events, food and drink, entertainment, transport services and links, types of accommodation, etc.) for the following destinations:

- Blackpool
- Newquay
- Snowdonia
- The New Forest
- Glasgow
- York
- Belfast
- Birmingham
- Aviemore
- Alton Towers Resort
- Chester
- Bath

The students' leaflets also need to explain what specific types of visitors each destination appeals to and why this is the case, e.g. families, groups, couples, families with young children, senior citizens, individuals, business travellers, visitors with specific needs, etc. Students' explanations will vary – the important point is that they are able to justify them adequately.

Topic 3.3: The impacts of tourism

Activity 1

a. Positive impacts of tourism suggested by students could include – creating jobs, providing income for tourist businesses, providing income for non-tourist businesses, improved facilities for visitors and local people, improved quality of life, better infrastructure (roads, railways, communications), awareness of other cultures, etc.

b. Negative impacts of tourism could include disruption and nuisance to local people, increase in prices (houses, food, services), more crime, prostitution, loss of local cultures, 'westernisation' in developing countries, hostility to tourists, environmental damage, etc.

c. After reading the information on Palma Nova, students are asked to highlight a range of positive impacts of tourism, including creating jobs in tourist attractions, accommodation and amenities aimed at holidaymakers, the fact that facilities built for tourists will benefit locals as well, increased income to the area that is re-spent on local goods and services (the 'multiplier effect'), improved infrastructure, etc.

d. Students read the extracts from members of different communities and are asked to identify key negative impacts that tourism can have on destination areas. These could include – increased racism, land conflicts between local people and tourism developers, increase in prostitution, disruption to traditional ways of life, changes to cultures, loss of traditional industries, over-reliance on tourism, increased crime, etc.

Activity 2

a. Students' answers will vary, but should reflect the following key points:

Regeneration: (1) Renewal of run-down urban areas; (2) Development of redundant buildings in the countryside; (3) Traditional buildings used for new activities, e.g. museums, art galleries, concert venues; (4) Money from tourism used in regeneration schemes.

Conservation: (1) Protection of wildlife and habitats; (2) Creation of National Parks, Heritage Coasts, Areas of Outstanding Natural Beauty (AONBs), nature reserves.

Creation of more parks, open spaces, etc. (1) Used by visitors and local people; (2) Supported by increased income from tourism.

Improved 'street furniture': (1) Local community as well as visitors benefit; (2) Tourism would decrease if destinations not well kept; (3) Supported by income from tourism; (4) Improved quality of life for local people.

b. Students use a variety of reference sources (the Internet, textbooks, etc.) to investigate the negative environmental impacts of tourism in one of the destinations listed. Their group presentations should cover a variety of issues, including loss of wildlife habitats, pollution in marine areas, erosion of footpaths, unsightly hotel developments, land taken for roads, car parks, etc.

Activity 3

After reading the scenario on the negative impacts of tourism, students present their work as meeting notes on how the impacts can be reduced and minimised. They will then feed their ideas back to the class and discuss the areas that they have all identified. Students' ideas will vary, but they need to make realistic comments and observations, offering ideas under each of the 4 areas. Examples could include: (1) Planning and legislation – banning high-rise hotel developments, encouraging development that is sympathetic with local environment, restricting the overuse of signposting; (2) Managing traffic – banning car parking in sensitive areas, introducing car-free zones, encouraging travel by public transport; (3) Managing visitors – training visitor guides, developing a tourist information centre; (4) Education – running workshops for local people on the economic importance of tourism, showing videos on flights to highlight to visitors the importance of respecting the environment and culture of the island, training tourist guides.

Activity 4

a. The International Ecotourism Society's definition of ecotourism is given on page 13. Another definition from the US-based Nature Conservancy is *'environmentally responsible travel to natural areas, in order to enjoy and appreciate nature (and accompanying cultural features, both past and present) that promote conservation, have a low visitor impact and provide for beneficially active socio-economic involvement of local peoples'.*

b. Students are to use the Internet, carrying out research to find out what different ecotourism products and services are available. Students must identify these products and briefly describe them. Results will vary, but are likely to focus on ecotourism holidays, activities such as whale watching, deep sea diving, coral reef tours, etc. An interesting point for discussion is the <u>location</u> of ecotourism activities. Most are found in exotic destinations overseas, but activities such as dolphin watching off the west Wales coast and other types of 'wildlife watching' in the UK can also be thought of as 'ecotourism'.

c. Students will use the information that they gathered in Tasks 4a and 4b, together with class notes and discussion, to complete the table in their books, which asks them to identify the advantages and disadvantages of ecotourism. Students' views will vary depending on class input, research and knowledge, but are likely to include the protection of wildlife and habitats, income from tourists, possible dangers to habitats, disruption to wildlife, etc.

Topic 3.4: The issue of sustainability

Activity 1a

After reading the account of the sustainable development initiative, students must answer a number of questions. Possible answers include:

i. To produce items using local materials (wool), while at the same time supporting local farmers and the rural economy.
ii. Increased income to local farmers; local produce and resources, thus reduction of carbon footprint; support networks develop; enables farmers to maintain their traditional industry.
iii. Only limited production – may not make a large impact overall, but could be a catalyst for further business development.
iv. Defra; the Yorkshire Dales sustainable development fund (SDF); Yorkshire Dales National Park.

Activity 1b

After reading the extract about sustainable tourism in the Red Sea, students must answer a number of questions.

i. Responses will vary, but students need to identify that the Red Sea area receives a large number of tourists every year and is a sensitive environment.
ii. Conservation, increased facilities for tourists, environmentally-sound developments, shared 'best practice', culture develops, education of visitors and local people on the importance of the environment, better signposting.
iii. Cost – who will pay? Will the plan continue over a long period of time? Will it attract even more tourists to an already fragile area?

Activity 2

a. Students work in small groups to discuss current transport issues that affect the leisure and tourism industries. These could include fuel prices, costs of different types of transport (air, rail, road, sea), environmental issues (carbon footprint), terrorist attacks, public transport provision (for accessing local leisure facilities), etc.

b. Based on the issues highlighted in task 2a, students must consider the ways in which each issue impacts on how leisure and tourism customers may choose to travel, i.e. choice of transport methods, safety and security of travel, 'green' alternatives for travel, etc.

c. Students are given information on one of the sustainability initiatives and must make a presentation to the rest of the class, after carrying out appropriate research.
d. This task involves the students visiting the relevant pages of the easyJet website and answering 5 questions:

i.   Carbon dioxide accounts for the majority of greenhouse gas emissions. You offset your emissions to support projects that help the environment.
ii. EasyJet is currently supporting the Perlabi Hydroelectric Plant – this is a small hydoelectric plant in Ecuador that uses water from the Chirizacha River. It is expected that, in the first 10 years of this project, its reduction in emissions will be 74,000 tonnes. This project reduces the reliance of fossil fuel power as well as offering jobs to the local community.
iii. Efficient use of their aircraft, new aircraft, only flying short-haul, avoiding congested hubs, only flying direct, short turnaround times at airports, have a simple airport infrastructure system, use less ground equipment, keep waste to a minimum, fly efficiently, etc.
iv. The carbon emissions for an easyJet flight from London Gatwick to Glasgow is 95.7g/km.
v.   Car = 104g/km; travelling with another airline = 121g/km.

Activity 3

a. Students are asked to imagine that they work at a large UK holiday centre. This could be a facility such as Butlin's, Center Parcs, a forest holiday centre or perhaps a large caravan park with indoor and outdoor facilities for guests. They must produce a poster that suggests ways in which the facility could be more 'green'. Suggested areas to consider include heating and lighting, suppliers, waste disposal and resources used.
b. Students are given details of one of the environmental award schemes mentioned in their books – Green Tourism Business Scheme www.green-business.co.uk, Europarc www.europarc.org or Green Destinations www.greendestinations.blogspot.com. They must research their scheme and produce a table showing its advantages and disadvantages for leisure and tourism organisations and destinations. Answers will vary, but are likely to include mention of protecting the environment and wildlife, attracting more visitors, helping communities to develop sustainable tourism businesses, etc.

Unit 4 Customers and employment in leisure and tourism

Topic 4.1: Visitor attractions, leisure facilities and tourist destinations

Activity 1

a. Students will list a variety of visitor attractions from around the world – built and natural. Their answers will vary dependent upon knowledge and experiences. The student may add to their list during feedback from this task.

b. Students then sort their list of attractions from Task 1a into those in the UK and those overseas.

c. Using the map on the relevant page of the Alton Towers website for reference, students are asked to identify all the different products and services that the attraction offers to visitors (not just the rides!). These include rides, hotels, the water park, golf course, first aid facilities, cash point machines, parking, toilets, gardens, catering outlets, shops, etc.

d. Students use their answers from Task 1c to produce a poster to advertise the products and services on offer at Alton Towers.

e. Working in groups, students must carry out some further research into Alton Towers to discover (1) Who the attraction appeals to; (2) Annual visitor numbers; (3) Why people visit the attraction. Students produce a written report to show their findings, which will vary depending on their research outcomes.

Activity 2

a. *UK leisure facilities* – examples include Ponds Forge Sports Centre Sheffield, Wembley Stadium, Spectrum Leisure Complex Guildford, Millennium Stadium Cardiff, Chessington World of Adventures. *International leisure facilities* – examples include Yellowstone National Park, Madison Square Garden in New York, Melbourne Cricket Ground (MCG), Disneyland Resort Paris, Whistler Resort in Canada.

b. After visiting a local leisure centre, students produce a leaflet describing all the different products and services on offer to visitors.

c. Results will vary depending on the actual leisure centre visited.

d. Ideas will vary, but could include discussion of longer opening hours, up-to-date activities, e.g. pilates, meeting government agenda, e.g. on fitness and health, higher quality provision, greater access by all members of society, e.g. disabled people.

e. Responses will vary depending on the actual leisure centre visited, but could include school children, sports groups, senior citizens, families, etc. Students must justify why the leisure centre appeals to the people they have identified.

Activity 3

a. Students locate the destinations on the outline map of the world as shown on page 28. Students could peer assess this exercise working in pairs.

b. Students choose one of the destinations from the map (Task 3a) to investigate in further detail and produce a mini-guide to the destination. Students' work will vary and may be limited in detail due to access to relevant information. You should direct students to OFFICIAL tourist board websites when gathering information for this task, since these are the most reliable and authoritative. The website www.towd.com Tourist Offices Worldwide Directory is a good starting point for this type of work, as is the World Travel Guide www.worldtravelguide.net.

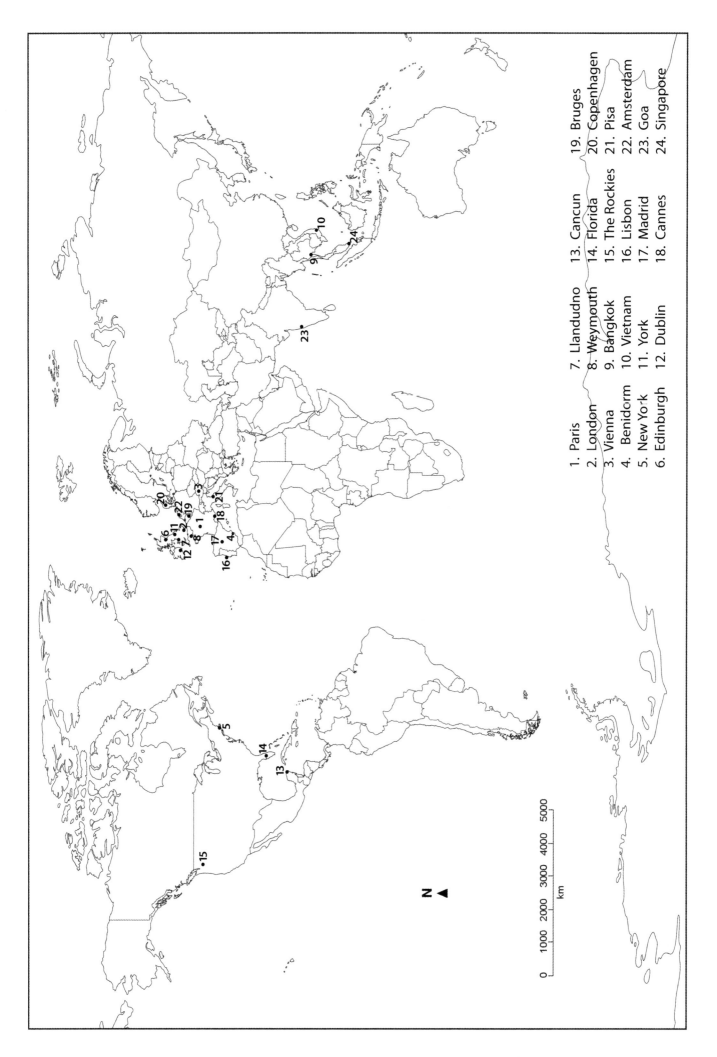

1. Paris
2. London
3. Vienna
4. Benidorm
5. New York
6. Edinburgh
7. Llandudno
8. Weymouth
9. Bangkok
10. Vietnam
11. York
12. Dublin
13. Cancun
14. Florida
15. The Rockies
16. Lisbon
17. Madrid
18. Cannes
19. Bruges
20. Copenhagen
21. Pisa
22. Amsterdam
23. Goa
24. Singapore

km
0 1000 2000 3000 4000 5000

N ◀

Topic 4.2: Customer choice

Activity 1

a. Many textbooks and Internet sites have definitions of 'leisure time'. Two examples are......'*Leisure or free time, is a period of time spent out of work and essential domestic activity. It is also the period of recreational and discretionary time before or after compulsory activities such as eating and sleeping, going to work or running a business, attending school and doing homework*' (Wikipedia)........'*Time outside of paid employment, at the disposal of the individual and during which time he or she has the freedom to choose what to do*' (Complete A-Z Travel & Leisure Handbook).
b. Students must identify the different activities that they like to do in their leisure time.
c. Students complete the table with the reasons for taking part in their leisure activities. Class discussion will be useful as an exchange of ideas for this task.
d. Unjumbled words are: age, culture, gender, household type, social group, specific needs, disposable income/finance.
e. Students must identify the key personal factors that they think would influence the person's choice of leisure activities (refer to Activity 4d for examples). Students' responses should include:

i. Gender, age, disposable income, household type;
ii. Age, gender, disposable income, social group;
iii. Specific needs, household type, disposable income;
iv. Specific needs, household type, social group;
v. Disposable income, household type, age;
vi. Household type, specific needs, culture.

Activity 2

Students are asked to identify the possible external factors affecting leisure choice for a range of scenarios. Answers include:

a. Availability of the facility;
b. Availability of public transport to facilities;
c. Current interests, fashions and trends;
d. Media influences;
e. Influence of others (family);
f. Time/work commitment.

Topic 4.3: Providing service for differing customer types and needs

Activity 1

Students should complete the wordsearch as shown on page 30, finding these different types of customers who take part in leisure and tourism activities – individuals, groups, different ages, different cultures, non-English speakers, business people, specific needs.

Activity 2

Students are required to identify possible customer needs for a range of scenarios. Answers include:

a. Speed of travel, quality of service, access to business facilities while travelling;
b. Good signage at the attractions, access to pre-visit information (brochures, website, etc.);

N	Q	S	D	J	Q	O	G	Q	L	J	I	H	B	S	D	U	O
F	O	L	D	M	O	J	S	O	X	R	Z	U	M	L	I	F	W
G	G	N	D	E	Q	V	G	N	U	O	S	T	E	A	F	S	Q
H	I	A	E	L	E	V	Y	P	R	I	L	S	U	U	F	R	Y
V	T	F	G	N	S	N	M	H	N	G	M	D	S	D	E	D	P
P	C	A	H	P	G	R	C	E	Q	L	B	T	O	I	R	F	J
C	W	Q	U	M	W	L	S	I	O	V	C	R	H	V	E	J	N
M	V	O	E	Z	M	S	I	C	F	U	D	K	L	I	N	N	Y
C	R	Z	G	X	P	E	K	S	I	I	A	C	W	D	T	O	U
G	M	D	X	E	R	M	F	R	H	M	C	S	W	N	C	X	L
E	S	C	O	Z	M	H	W	J	O	S	Q	E	L	I	U	Z	D
Z	O	P	M	Z	N	U	M	D	W	R	P	J	P	H	L	I	N
G	L	S	U	E	O	F	K	I	I	I	A	E	V	S	T	F	Z
E	N	F	M	C	Q	U	K	T	S	P	T	I	A	E	U	Z	T
S	E	G	A	T	N	E	R	E	F	F	I	D	D	K	R	R	B
A	B	A	T	Y	S	C	T	I	N	A	E	C	M	N	E	X	N
R	U	R	K	L	K	G	T	Q	L	O	O	A	B	R	S	R	X
G	Z	L	G	Q	T	R	C	O	S	R	S	B	N	T	H	I	S

c.   Speed of travel, access to information, accessibility to services and facilities;

d.   Different types of equipment needed in their accommodation (highchair, pushchair, play equipment, etc.);

e.   Students' responses will vary, but should take into account their answers to Tasks 2a - 2d.

Activity 3

Students either need to visit a local hotel or leisure centre, or have listened to a guest speaker, in order to complete this task. They must produce a staff booklet concerning health and safety in the facility, providing detailed information on the 4 sections listed in their books. Students' booklets will vary, but must include key elements of information gathered from the visit or talk.

Activity 4

a.   Many textbooks and Internet sites have definitions of 'customer service'. Two examples are......'*Customer service (also known as client service) is the provision of service to customers before, during and after a purchase*'

(Wikipedia)……..'*Customer service concerns all aspects of the interface between a customer and an organisation* (Complete A-Z Travel & Leisure Handbook).

b. Students work in pairs to carry out a variety of role plays. For each situation, students must consider how to use customer service to meet the needs of their customers. The rest of the class should make notes on the performance of the member of staff and customer, in order to take part in a class discussion at the end of the task.

i. Key points to consider – agree contact details with customer, agree all details of the honeymoon package only with the husband-to-be;

ii. Key points to consider – remain calm at all times, confirm that the customer's points are valid, try to arrange another appropriate room, keep the customer informed at all times, complete necessary paperwork for head office;

iii. Key points to consider – explain all procedures in detail to the customer, be aware of health and safety issues, answer all questions appropriately, oversee customer when carrying out activities.

c. Answers may include – repeat customers, increased profits, good reputation, happy and motivated staff, low staff turnover, increased sales, low levels of complaints, etc.

Activity 5

a. The term 'culture' has a number of meanings. Most commonly, it represents the common attitudes, beliefs and customs that characterises a group of people or an organisation. It can also refer to excellence in taste, for example in fine arts and humanities. In leisure and tourism, recognising and respecting cultural differences is important in, for example, delivering leisure activities and developing tourism destinations.

b. Students are asked to imagine that they work as cabin crew for British Airways and must explain how passengers' different cultural needs must be considered and accommodated in a range of scenarios:

i. *Religious beliefs* – opportunities and facilities for prayer, seating arrangements on aircraft and in terminals, passenger segregation, etc.

ii. *Dietary requirements* – meals for special diets, timings of meals, fasting, etc.

iii. *Customs and traditions* – segregation, seating arrangements, gender issues, etc.

iv. *Behaviour and dress code* – expected behaviour related to nationalities, gender issues, respectful and appropriate cabin crew dress, etc.

v. *Different languages* – speaking more than one language, availability of interpreters, printed items and announcements in multiple languages, etc.

c. Students' suggestions will vary, but are likely to focus on pricing policies (discounts for certain groups and individuals), the range of activities available, facilities available, opening times, outreach work in schools and community groups, menus available in food outlets, changing facilities, etc.

d. Students use the 4 headings in this task to write a proposal for a culturally-sound hotel for the 21st century and beyond. Responses will vary, but students should be encouraged to refer back to the answers they gave for Tasks 5a – 5c as a starting point. All parts of their written proposal must be justified.

Activity 6

i. Clear signage, availability of printed materials in large print and braille, audio information devices, welcome for assistance dogs, etc.

ii. Access ramps, widened access to facilities, lifts, availability of wheelchairs, disabled parking spaces, etc.

iii. Changing facilities, bottle and food warming on offer, high chairs, feeding rooms, etc.

iv. Clear menus, choices at meal times, information leaflets, etc.

v. Facilities to store medication securely, private areas for administering medication, knowledge of common conditions, oxygen availability, etc.

Topic 4.4: Employment opportunities in leisure and tourism

Activity 1

a. Students are asked to define what is meant by 'qualities', giving an example of a quality that they think is important to be able to work in leisure and tourism. A definition could include the fact that qualities are characteristics that individuals possess, such as enthusiasm, patience, empathy, confidence, etc. Qualities also refer to a person's personality, which could be outgoing, reserved, lively, quiet, etc. Students should recognise that qualities can be both positive and negative. Students will have their own views on which quality is important to be able to work in leisure and tourism. They must be able to justify what they say on this topic.

b. Students are asked to define what is meant by 'skills', giving an example of a skill that is commonly required by people working in leisure and tourism. Skills are generally what people learn to do, e.g. dealing with customers (customer service), keyboard skills, learning a language, operating plant and machinery at a leisure centre, selling, etc. Students will give different answers when asked to give an example of a skill commonly required to work in leisure and tourism. They must be able to justify what they say on this topic.

c. Examples of *skills* needed to work in leisure and tourism include – ICT, languages, ticketing, customer service, keyboard skills, teamwork skills, numeracy, literacy, presentation skills, etc. Examples of *qualities* needed to work in leisure and tourism include – confidence, patience, independence, diplomacy, critical thinking, problem solving, etc.

d. Main duties are: (1) Induction of new members; (2) Designing fitness programmes; (3) Cleaning and maintenance of equipment; (4) Dealing with enquiries; (5) Working as a personal trainer; (6) Helping to increase membership numbers and income.

e. Students should highlight – motivated, committed, outgoing, offer high levels of customer service, enjoy working with the public, ICT literate, be able to use fitness equipment, flexible, have sound basic skills, level 2 qualification in fitness and exercise, first aid qualification, etc.

f. Students' job advertisements will vary, but must include the relevant skills, qualities and qualifications needed for this type of job. Students may like to refer to the job description on page 104 of their books when completing this task.

Activity 2

a. Students must read through the 3 job advertisements with a view to applying for the job that interests them most.

b. Students produce a letter of application for the job, using the guidelines given in their books. They should be encouraged to include 'action' words in their letters, e.g. achieved, introduced, set up, developed, created, completed, etc.

c. A CV must be produced by each student. CVs vary in style, but must include relevant basic information, e.g. full name, postal address, contact telephone number(s), nationality, education to date (most recent first), academic and vocational qualifications, employment history (if any), skills and achievements, interests, referees. Again, 'action' words are useful when writing a CV.

d. Students conduct role plays of jobs interviews, taking turns at playing the interviewer and interviewee. These could be video recorded for discussion and analysis.

Sample assessment material

Unit 1: The leisure and tourism industry

Answer the following questions which test your knowledge and understanding of Unit 1. Marks awarded for each question are shown in brackets, e.g. (2).

1(a) Which of the following is a key component of the leisure industry? (tick **one** box)

     ☐ Tourist information

     ☐ Countryside recreation

     ☐ Transportation

     ☐ Travel agents   (1)

1(b) Identify **two** further key components of the leisure industry

i)...

ii).. (2)

1(c) A package holiday is a type of holiday taken by tourists. Define the term 'package' and give an example of a typical package holiday destination:

Definition..

....

.... (2)

Example .... (1)

1(d) State **two** duties of air cabin crew

....

.... (2)

1(e) Visitor attractions can be either natural or built. Identify **one** natural and **one** built attraction that can be found in the UK:

Natural ....

Built .... (2)

1(f) Read through the following information about The City Tour Bus before answering the question that follows:

The City Tour Bus

The City Tour Bus is a new sightseeing bus company which has set up in key tourist towns and cities. The hop-on, hop-off bus tour offers a guided tour of the city for tourists of all ages and nationalities. The service is available from June through to August.

Tourists pay one price for a one-day ticket and can hop-on and off the bus as and when they wish. Buses leave from the main departure point hourly.

Every bus has its own guide who will provide a commentary in both English and a key language (French, Spanish or German). The guides are from the local area and have been on an intensive training course in order to equip them to answer customer questions.

For the younger passenger, The City Tour Bus provides an activity pack to be completed during the tour, with prizes available and awarded by the guide.

Evaluate the advantages and disadvantages of The City Tour Bus:

....

....

....

....

....

....

....

.... (5)

Question 1 Total = 15 marks

2(a) Which of the following is a functional area of a leisure and tourism organisation?

☐ Travel agents

☐ Sales and marketing

☐ Manager

☐ Reception   (1)

2(b) All leisure and tourism organisations set aims and objectives. Identify **one** financial and **one** not-for-profit aim of leisure and tourism companies:

Financial aim ....

Not-for-profit aim... (2)

2(c) Explain **two** different ways that a travel agent could use e-mail as a new technology to improve service to its customers.

....

....

....

.... (4)

2(d) Below are statements about Dover Castle in Kent. Complete the table by matching the statement to the correct element of the marketing mix:

Information statement	Element of the marketing mix
Located in south-east England	
Adults £9.50 Children £6.00 Senior Citizens £7.25	
Listen to our radio advert for more details	
The tunnels are open daily and offer the opportunity to experience what life was really like for our soldiers.	

(4)

2(e) Read the following information about Health and Safety legislation affecting employees before answering the question that follows.

General duties of an employer to their employees:

- It is an employer's duty to ensure the health, safety and welfare of their employees;
- It is the employer's duty to ensure that equipment is safe and does not pose a risk to an employee's health;
- To provide information, training and instruction to employees to ensure the health and safety of employees;
- To provide a working environment that is safe for all employees.

(Adapted from the Health and Safety at Work Act 1974).

Identify **three** ways that a leisure centre could comply with this legislation.

1..

2..

3... (3)

Question 2 total = 14 marks

3(a) Give **one** reason why someone may visit a spa for the weekend.

…… (1)

3(b) Read this short extract before answering the question that follows.

The Fox family from Bristol are going to be spending the weekend away in Canterbury so that they can attend their nephew and cousins' birthday party.

What is their main reason for travel?

…… (1)

3(c) There are several different transport methods that a family could use to travel to France. Explain **two** factors that people would consider when choosing which transport method they will use.

Factor 1……

……..

……..

Factor 2……

……..

…… (4)

3(d) Describe **two** methods of security currently used at airports in the fight against terrorism.

Method 1………..

……

……

Method 2………

……..

…… (4)

Question 3 Total = 10 marks

4(a) Give **one** example of a UK seaside resort.

…… (1)

4(b) Describe **one** positive impact that tourists visiting a seaside resort could have upon the community.

....

....

.... (2)

4(c) Describe **one** negative impact that tourism may have upon a seaside resort.

....

....

.... (2)

4(d) Explain what is meant by 'ecotourism'.

....

.... (2)

4(e) Describe **two** key features of a purpose-built tourist destination.

Feature 1..

....

.... (2)

Feature 2..

....

.... (2)

Question 4 Total = 11 marks

Sample assessment material — ANSWERS

Unit 1: The leisure and tourism industry

1(a) Countryside recreation (1)

1(b) Any two from:

- Sport and physical recreation
- Arts and entertainment
- Home-based leisure
- Play and activity based leisure (2)

1(c) Definition: A holiday that contains two elements or more sold at a set price (2).
Any relevant example of a typical package holiday destination, e.g. Benidorm, Magaluf, Palma Nova, etc. (1).

1(d) Any two from:

- Ensure passenger health and safety
- To serve meals and drinks
- To meet customer needs
- To sell duty free goods
- To carry out basic safety checks (2)

1(e) 1 mark for a relevant UK built attraction, e.g. Legoland Windsor, Alton Towers; 1 mark for a relevant UK natural attraction, e.g. Lake District National Park, Sherwood Forest (2).

NB Do not allow marks for beach or theme park, the student should name the attraction.

1(f) *Advantages*: hop-on, hop-off, pay one price for all-day ticket, regular departures, guide (speaks French, Spanish and German), activity packs for children.
Disadvantages: what if you do not speak English, French, Spanish or German?, quality of the guides as training seems limited, only a limited season.

Students will need to evaluate each point as to why it is an advantage or disadvantage to gain the full 5 marks. A maximum of 3 marks can be awarded for correct identification of the advantages and disadvantages (5).

Question 1 Total = 15 marks

2(a) Sales and marketing (1)

2(b) *Financial aim*: to increase profits, to increase sales, to maximise profit, to increase market share (1).
Not-for-profit aim: to provide for the community, to meet environmental standards, to support local or national charities (1).

2(c) The travel agent could e-mail customers informing them of late deals, discounts and other special offers available (2). Confirmation of bookings – travel agents could e-mail confirmation of bookings to the customers instead of having to write letters (2).

1 mark for the correct identification of a reasonable way of using e-mail and 1 mark for a suitable explanation.

2(d)

Information statement	Element of the marketing mix
Located in south-east England	Place
Adults £9.50 Children £6.00 Senior Citizens £7.25	Price
Listen to our radio advert for more details	Promotion
The tunnels are open daily and offer the opportunity to experience what life was really like for our soldiers.	Product

(4)

2(e)

1. Regularly check equipment that is used by employees
2. Provide induction training for all new staff at the centre
3. Maintain the working environment to a high standard

Award marks for any valid answer to a maximum of (3)

Question 2 Total = 14 marks

3(a) Relaxation (1)

3(b) Visiting friends and relatives (1)

3(c)
Factor 1: *Cost* – people may have a tight budget and therefore the cost of each method of transport will be important. They may be looking for the cheapest method.
Factor 2: *Frequency of services* – travellers may choose a transport method that offers a choice of times when they can travel. This is often the case for business travellers who may need to travel at short notice.

1 mark for the correct identification of factor and 1 mark for a valid explanation to a maximum of (4)

3(d)
Method 1: The ban on liquids in hand luggage – people cannot take liquids in their hand luggage apart from some specified items such as baby milk.

Method 2: Facial scanning – a picture is taken as you enter passport control and checked against you as you enter the gate.

Award marks for any valid answer to a maximum of (4)

Question 3 Total = 10 marks

4(a) Brighton, Southend-on-Sea, Skegness, Blackpool, Weymouth, Bournemouth, Great Yarmouth… or any relevant example (1)

4(b) Facilities built for tourists can also be used by the local community. Improved 'street furniture', i.e. better signposting, floral displays, etc. Jobs will be created with more businesses opening and more visitors using existing businesses. Locals could be employed (2).

4(c) Overcrowding – in the summer months the town is likely to get very busy, which will affect the quality of life of the local people (2). Other ideas could include: congestion, increased pollution, inflation, increased crime. A suitable description will be awarded 2 marks.

4(d) A coherent definition which contains key elements of – environmentally-responsible travel, promoting conservation, low visitor impact, providing benefits for local communities (2)

4(e)
Feature 1: Accommodation in the form of hotels, chalets or apartments will be available for visitors (2)
Feature 2: Catering facilities such as restaurants, cafés and takeaways will be available for the guests (2)

Other features may include: shops, play areas, leisure facilities.

Question 4 Total = 11 marks

Sample assessment material

Unit 2: Sales, promotion and operations in leisure and tourism

The assessment for this unit is a series of tasks that students carry out under the direction and control of their teacher(s). The following tasks are designed to give you practice in completing a controlled assessment.

You will be assessed on these tasks using the following criteria:

Assessment criteria	Applies to these tasks
Planning and research	Tasks 1, 2 & 4
Presenting information	Tasks 1, 2 & 4
Planning and design	Task 3
Producing material	Task 3
Evaluation and suggesting improvements	Tasks 2 & 3

Task 1: (12 marks)

Choose a leisure organisation such as a leisure centre, sports centre, cinema, theatre, etc. for this task.

You must investigate the sales and marketing mix for your chosen leisure organisation, producing a written report to show your findings.

This report should include the following information:

* Selling situations which occur at the organisation;
* The departments within the organisation that support sales;
* The aims and objectives of the organisation;
* Key features of the products/services that the organisation sells;
* Prices of the products/services;
* Where the organisation is located.

Task 2: (18 marks)

Choose a tourism organisation such as a travel agent, airline, hotel, visitor attraction, etc. for this task.

You must carry out an evaluation of the promotional techniques and materials used by your chosen organisation, suggesting possible ways in which these could be improved.

The evaluations should be displayed through annotation of the promotional materials/techniques. Your evaluations should use the following headings:

* Design;
* Placement (e.g. where an advertisement is placed);

- Size and scale of the promotions;
- Target market for the promotion;
- Suitability for the identified target market.

For each of the promotional techniques/materials you have evaluated you must suggest improvements that could realistically be made and justify these suggestions.

Task 3: (18 marks)

You must design a piece of promotional material for a chosen leisure or tourism organisation.

You work must include the following:

- A stated target market for your piece of promotional material;
- A plan and design for your piece of promotional material;
- Your finished piece of promotional material;
- An evaluation of your piece of promotional material, to include – how the promotional material meets the target market, how effectively the information is displayed and suggested improvements you would make if you were to produce this again.

Task 4: (12 marks)

For this task, you must choose a leisure or tourism organisation that uses, or has available, new technology.

You are to produce a presentation that:

- Identifies the new technology;
- Describes the new technology;
- Explains the impact that this new technology is having/has had on the operations of the business.

Sample assessment material

Unit 3: The leisure and tourism environment

Answer the following questions which test your knowledge and understanding of Unit 3. Marks awarded for each question are shown in brackets, e.g. (2).

1(a) New technology influences the development of products and services in leisure and tourism. Recently there has been a huge increase in home-based leisure.

Which of the technologies below has developed as a result of this increase? (Tick **one** box)

☐ GPS

☐ E-tickets

☐ Nintendo Wii

☐ Automated check-in (1)

1(b) Name **two** other factors/trends that have influenced the development of the leisure and tourism industry, other than technology.

i)...

ii).. (2)

1(c) A large number of transport operators have introduced automated check-in. Define what this means and then give **one** advantage of this to the transport companies and **one** advantage of this to the customer.

Definition..

....

.... (2)

Advantage to the company .... (1)

Advantage to the customer .... (1)

1(d) Explain how consumer tastes have changed over recent years in relation to leisure and tourism. In your answer you could include reference to:

- Environment
- Expected standards
- Experiences sought
- Popular products and services
- Any other relevant points

....

....

....

....

....

....

....

.... (6)

Question 1 Total = 13 marks

2(a) In which county is Brighton located? (Tick **one** box)

☐ Kent

☐ West Sussex

☐ Surrey

☐ Hampshire   (1)

2(b) Complete the following table by naming each of the destinations labelled A – F on the map of the UK on page 45 (6)

Label	Destination
A	
B	
C	
D	
E	
F	

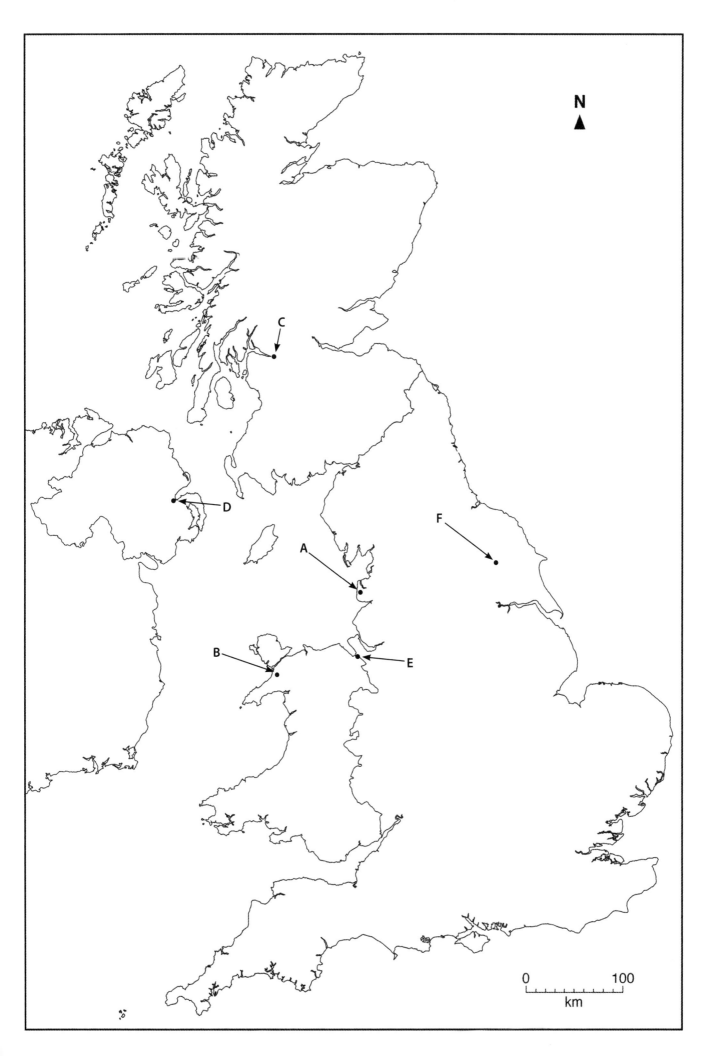

2(c) Explain the issues concerning transport links and routes into and around popular historical and cultural destinations such as York.

……..

……

……

……… (3)

2(d) Explain why Alton Towers appeals to families.

……

……

……

……

……… (3)

2(e) Explain the role of a tourist board.

……

……

……… (2)

Question 2 Total = 15 marks

3(a) Identify **one** positive impact of tourism on a local community.

……… (1)

3(b) Read the extract below about the Glastonbury Festival before answering the question that follows.

Glastonbury is the largest green field performing arts and music festival in the world. It is held over 5 days each summer on farmland in the countryside area of Glastonbury. The festival has a wide range of events, music stages and activities to participate in, as well as offering space for the festival goers to camp. Thousands of visitors flock to Glastonbury each year to see a wide range of acts take to the stage throughout the days and evenings.

Explain **one** reason why you think this festival takes place in the countryside.

……

……… (2)

Analyse the impacts (positive and negative) that the Glastonbury Festival may have upon the environment and local community.

....

....

....

....

....

....

....

....

....

....

.... (6)

Explain **one** possible method that could be used to reduce the negative impacts you have identified above.

....

.... (2)

Question 3 Total = 11 marks

4(a) Explain what is meant by 'sustainable development'.

.... (1)

4(b) Read the following extract before answering the question that follows.

My other car is a bus

Towards the end of 2004, Transport for London launched a £2 million advertising campaign entitled 'My other car is a bus'. This 3-month campaign was aimed primarily at families and school children in an attempt to ease suburban congestion and highlight the fact that a bus can be used instead of a car. The then Mayor of London, Ken Livingstone, said 'By making more bus journeys, and reducing car congestion, people can help to make London a cleaner, safer and more pleasant city'.

Evaluate the advantages and disadvantages of this campaign.

....

....

....

....

....

.... (5)

4(c) Read the following information before answering the question that follows.

The Green Tourism Business Scheme (GBTS)

The GTBS is a certification scheme for businesses. Businesses looking to join the scheme are assessed in a variety of ways with regard to their 'greenness'. Areas that are assessed include – energy use and water efficiency, using environmentally friendly goods and waste management. After the assessment, the business will receive either a bronze, silver or gold award depending on their level of achievement.

Evaluate the advantages and disadvantages of joining the GTBS if you were the owner of a small to medium-sized hotel.

....

....

....

....

....

....

.... (5)

Question 4 Total = 11 marks

Sample assessment material – ANSWERS

Unit 3: The leisure and tourism environment

1(a) Nintendo Wii (1)

1(b) Any two from:

- Changing tastes
- Changing lifestyles
- Changes to holiday patterns
- Ageing of the population (growth of 'silver surfers')
- Changes to family patterns
- Changing appeal of cruising (2)

1(c) Definition to include aspects of: Self check-in without a member of staff present, checking in using a machine, entering flight details to gain a boarding pass and other relevant statements (2).

Advantage to the company: cuts costs of fully staffing check-in, etc. (1)
Advantage to the customer: saves time at check-in, etc. (1)

1(d) A coherent explanation may include elements of:

- People are more environmentally-aware and so choose transport that is lower in carbon emissions and resorts that are eco friendly
- Consumer expectations have increased with more experience of travel and so higher standards are expected
- People are more concerned about health and fitness, resulting in new activities and active tourism products
- Many consumers are no longer thrilled by a package abroad, but are looking for something different such as adventure tourism
- People are working harder and therefore relaxation is paramount, leading to a growth in spa resorts, etc. (6)

A maximum of 3 marks awarded for simply a list of factors.

Question 1 Total = 13 marks

2(a) West Sussex (1)

2(b) One mark (maximum 6) for each correct location as follows:

Label	Destination
A	Blackpool
B	Snowdonia
C	Glasgow
D	Belfast
E	Chester
F	York

2(c) Explanation should include reference to traffic congestion, old style roads, lack of by-passes due to historical buildings and city walls, park-and-ride schemes, promotion of public transport, walking and cycling, etc. (3).

2(d) Explanation to include; wide range of rides and attractions aimed at different ages groups, varying entertainment, accommodation suitable for families, water park on site and any other relevant points (3).

2(e) To promote its designated area and support the development of the tourism industry (2).

Question 2 Total = 15 marks

3(a) Any one of: improve transport services, provide better access to leisure facilities, improved quality of life, employment opportunities, improved awareness of other cultures, etc. (1).

3(b) Explanation surrounding any of the following: space, access for visitors, cost (2).

Analyse the impacts (positive and negative) that the Glastonbury Festival may have upon the environment and local community.

For full marks students must produce an analysis. Answers may include:

* Increased employment in the area for the duration of the festival
* Congestion from increased traffic in a rural setting
* Noise pollution from the music all day and into the night
* Increased revenue to the area's businesses for the duration of the festival
* Increased crime and vandalism caused by festival goers

(6)

Explain one possible method that could be used to reduce the negative impacts you have identified above. Ideas could include:

* Limit access by car
* Education about the area
* Limit times for performances

(2)

Question 3 Total = 11 marks

4(a) Answers are likely to include reference to: preserving the environment for future generations, using resources wisely, etc. (1).

4(b) Answers may include:

* High cost to local government – money could be spent on improving transport
* Raises awareness of car usage
* May get people to use the bus for short journeys
* Congestion may be reduced as a result of the campaign
* Could improve air quality in London

(5)

4(c) Answers may include:

* Is it worth the cost for the potential increase in business?
* May attract a different type of tourist
* The tourists visiting may be willing to pay a little more to be 'green'
* Will be costly for the hotel to install all the measures required to meet the criteria?
* Will get more support in terms of promotion?
* May raise the profile of the business
* May give the business a new 'angle' from which to base its promotion

(5)

Question 4 Total = 11 marks

Sample assessment material

Unit 4: Customers and employment in leisure and tourism

The assessment for this unit is a series of tasks that students carry out under the direction and control of their teacher(s). The following tasks are designed to give you practice in completing a controlled assessment.

You will be assessed on these tasks using the following criteria:

Assessment criteria	Applies to these tasks
Planning and research	Tasks 2, 3 & 4
Presenting information	Tasks 1, 2 & 4
Planning and design	Task 1
Producing material	Task 3
Evaluation and suggesting improvements	Tasks 2 & 3

To carry out Tasks 1 and 2, you must choose **two** different examples from the list below. One example will be used to complete Task 1 and the other example used to complete Task 2:

* A visitor attraction in the UK;
* A visitor attraction overseas;
* A tourist destination in the UK;
* A tourist destination overseas;
* A leisure facility in the UK;
* A leisure facility overseas.

You must carry out research and gather information from more than one source when completing these tasks.

Task 1: (12 marks)

For your chosen example, investigate the products and services that the example offers, and how these appeal to its visitors/customers. This should be produced as a detailed poster or leaflet, which must include:

* The range of products/services provided;
* Customer needs of those who use/visit the example;
* How customer feedback is measured;
* The importance of customer service to the example.

Task 2: (18 marks)

For your second example, you must produce a written report which evaluates the reasons why people choose to visit the attraction/destination/facility in their leisure time.

When writing your report you will need to consider:

* The factors that influence a customer's choice;
* Personal and external factors that influence people's decision to visit your chosen example;
* The visitor trends, appeal and popularity of your chosen example.

Task 3: (18 marks)

You must use the example you have researched for either Task 1 or Task 2 to complete this activity.

Investigate the way that your chosen example provides service for a range of customer types and needs. This should be presented as a written report and will need to consider:

- What is meant by customer service;
- Which customer types visit the attraction/destination/facility.

Evaluate how successful your example is at meeting customer needs, by producing a magazine article that will be included in the trade and consumer press.

The evaluation should consider:

- How customer needs are met;
- How the staff are trained;
- How the example handles complaints;
- The strengths and weaknesses of the customer service provided.

Task 4: (12 marks)

Choose a UK or overseas visitor attraction or a UK or overseas leisure facility for this task.

You work in the human resources department of your example. You have been briefed to produce a new guide to employment within your attraction/facility. Your guide should include the following sections:

- The range of jobs available at your example, including the roles and responsibilities, skills and qualities required for the jobs;
- What makes a successful application (e.g. CV, interview skills, etc.);
- The staff induction that your example offers.

Skills Grid

Activity	Identify, gather & record relevant information and evidence	Analyse issues & problems	Analyse & evaluate evidence	Make reasoned judgements & present conclusions	Plan investigations and/or tasks	Carry out investigations and/or tasks	Numeracy	Literacy	ICT	Peer teaching & learning	Team working	Moral and ethical issues	Map skills	Decision making	Research skills	Presentation skills
Unit 1.1 1																
2								X								
3								X					X	X		
4	X		X			X	X	X	X				X	X		
5				X				X								
6								X								
7								X							X	
8	X							X		X						X
Unit 1.2 1								X								
2								X								
3						X		X	X		X	X		X		X
4					X	X		X			X					
5						X		X								
Unit 1.3 1								X								
2								X						X		
3								X								
Unit 1.4 1	X					X		X	X			X		X	X	X
2	X			X		X		X				X				X
3	X							X								
4			X	X		X		X								X
5				X		X		X								X
Unit 2.1 1				X	X			X	X					X	X	X
2																
Unit 2.2 1				X	X					X				X		X
2														X		X
Unit 2.3 1				X		X									X	
2				X										X		X
3																
Unit 2.4 1		X				X										
2											X			X		
3		X												X		X

Activity	Identify, gather & record relevant information and evidence	Analyse issues & problems	Analyse & evaluate evidence	Make reasoned judgements & present conclusions	Plan investigations and/or tasks	Carry out investigations and/or tasks	Numeracy	Literacy	ICT	Peer teaching & learning	Team working	Moral and ethical issues	Map skills	Decision making	Research skills	Presentation skills
Unit 3.1 1	X	X		X	X	X		X	X	X	X					X
2						X		X								
3	X	X			X	X		X		X	X					X
Unit 3.2 1	X							X					X		X	X
Unit 3.3 1	X	X		X				X				X				X
2	X	X				X		X			X	X				
3									X							
4	X							X								
Unit 3.4 1								X				X				
2	X	X		X	X			X				X			X	X
3	X	X		X	X	X						X				X
Unit 4.1 1	X					X		X	X	X	X		X			X
2					X		X	X					X			X
3					X			X								
Unit 4.2 1								X	X							
2								X								
Unit 4.3 1								X	X			X				X
2								X			X					X
3	X					X		X			X					X
4								X				X				X
5								X				X				X
6																
Unit 4.4 1						X		X						X	X	X
2																X

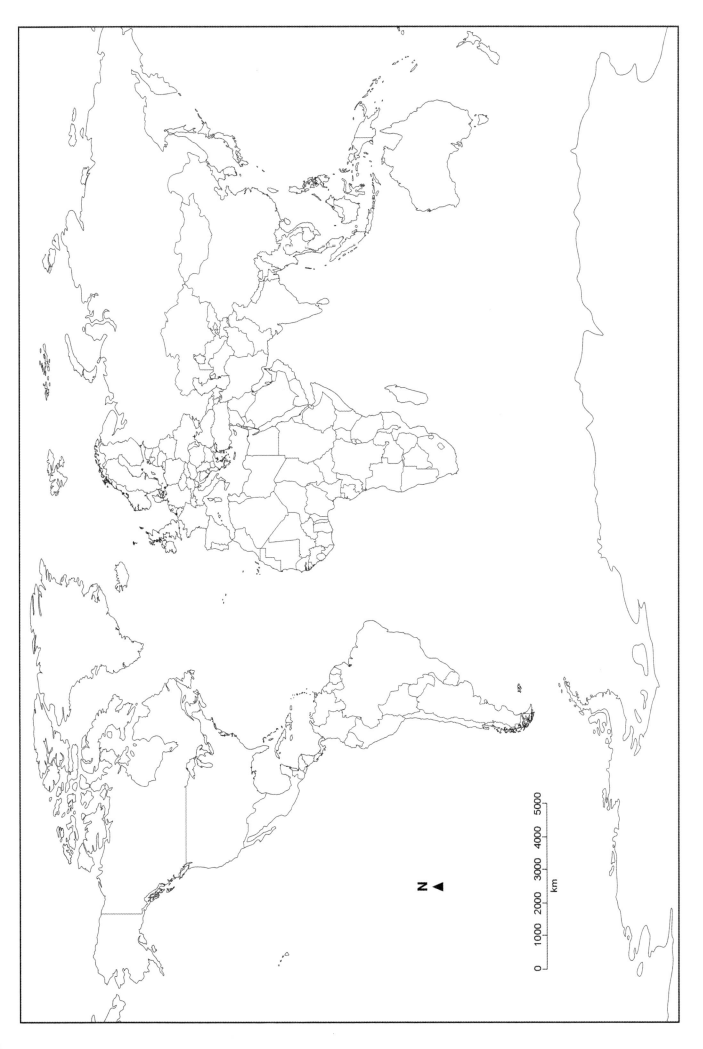

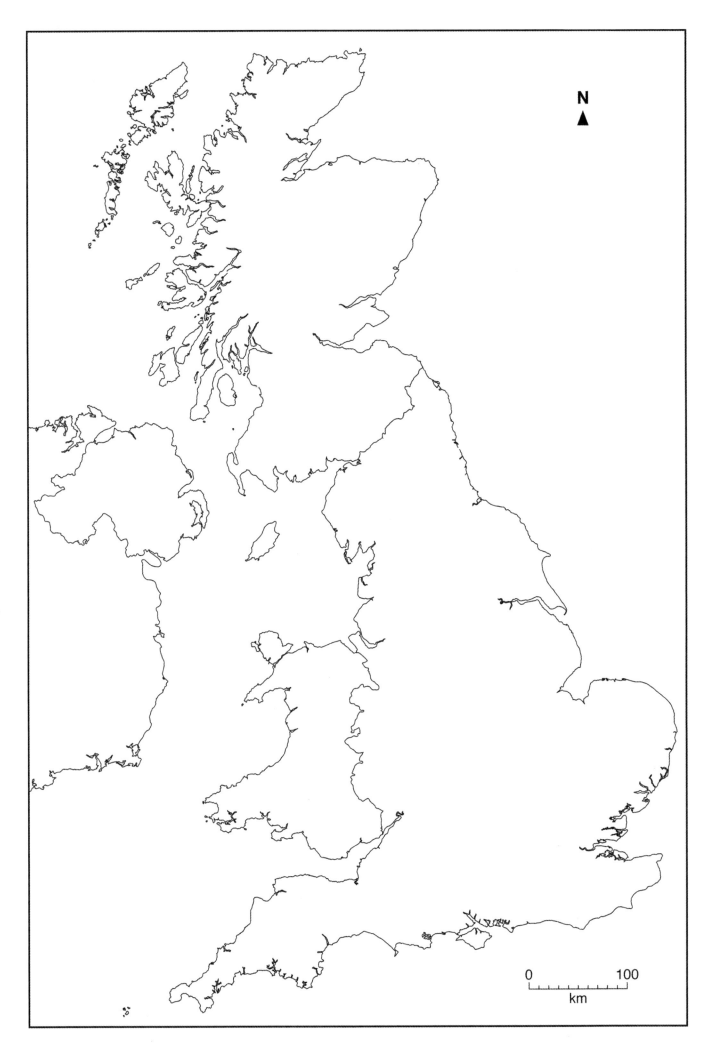

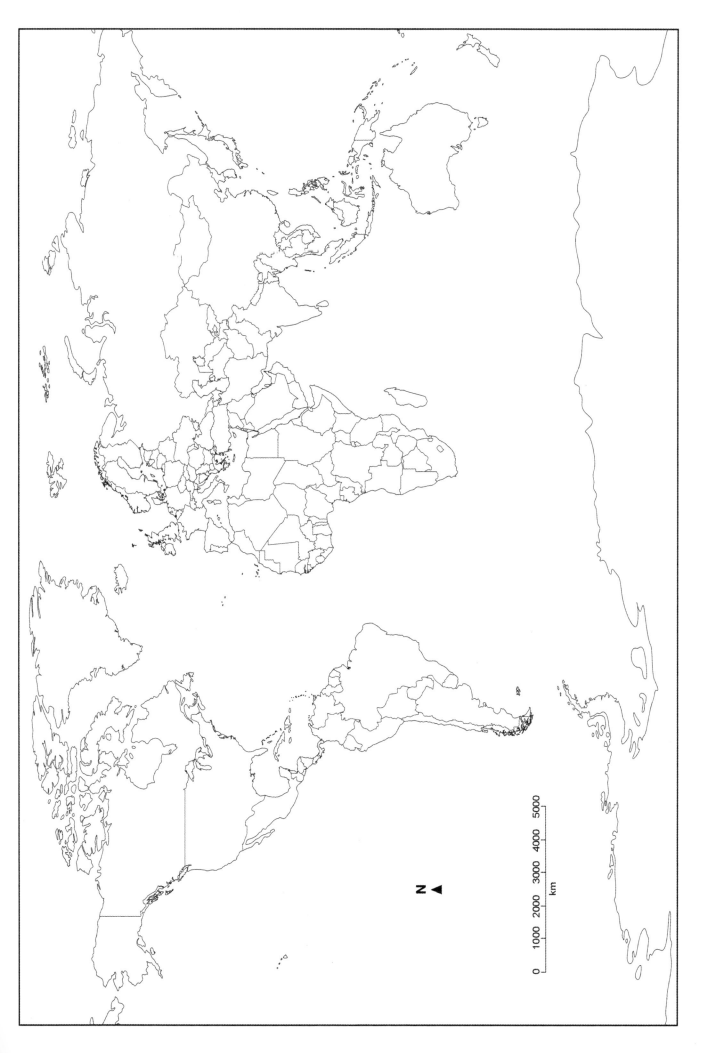

km

0   1000   2000   3000   4000   5000

N

0   100

km